PANORAMAS OF LONDON

PANORAMAS OF LONDON

TEXT BY ROWAN MOORE • PHOTOGRAPHS BY SAMPSON LLOYD

WEIDENFELD AND NICOLSON, LONDON

CONTENTS

INTRODUCTION

IMPRESSED into the fabric of London, just north of Leicester Square, is Notre Dame de France, a cylindrical post-war church decorated by Jean Cocteau. It is typical of London in several ways. It is unexpected and a little odd, it serves one of many foreign communities and its façade only vaguely suggests its remarkable interior. But its particular interest lies in its circular shape which does not, as one might expect of a church, signify eternity or perfection, but is the trace of a panorama built in 1791.

These structures were static, cumbersome and rather less suspenseful precursors of the cinema. Spectators placed in the centre of the space found themselves immersed in a realistic, 360 degree, painted image fixed to its walls. The idea was to create as complete and convincing a representation as was then possible. A favourite subject for panoramas were views of London, from the top of St Paul's, from a balloon or from the eye of a fictional bird extraordinarily skilled at drawing.

This could be seen as a last attempt to embrace the ever-expanding city in a single view before it bounded over the horizon into endless suburbs. For sixteenth- and seventeenth-century view-makers, the whole of London could be seen from an imaginary point slightly elevated above Southwark, and fitted into an elongated rectangle. Now you need a satellite. The panorama is also the most extreme example of an art-form that has always favoured London – the cityscape.

The typical view of Paris, for example, is taken from, along or into a boulevard. It depicts urban life from the viewpoint of a participant. The typical view of London, whether by Canaletto, Monet or André Derain, is by an outsider, and from a viewpoint that is both apart from the city proper and close to nature, like a hill or a bridge. London is portrayed almost as if it were a natural event, a piece of landscape. Similar positions are favoured by writers: the most famous poem about London, Wordsworth's 'Composed upon Westminster Bridge', is both taken from a detached position and is by a poet who more commonly drew his inspiration from nature.

In such views the city is inhabited not so much by people as by atmosphere. Many cities are best summed up by their most famous and vivacious streets or squares; not so London, where such spaces range from the dull (Parliament Square) to the unspeakable (Oxford Street). What does pervade and unify

ART CENTER COLLEGE OF DESIGN

London is its shifting light, the joint creation of the protean English weather and the fumes of the city. Canaletto preferred to depict its serene mode, and not only because of his Venetian bias: the light really can be that clear. Monet liked its fogginess. Derain extrapolated an explosive Fauve palette from its dramatic changes. Constable, painting on Hampstead Heath, omitted people, buildings and trees and depicted only clouds. Again, writers found the same inspiration as painters: Dickens's *Bleak House* opens with a pages-long reverie on fog.

The view of London as countryside by other means is not only a conceit of writers and artists. Rather, they are observing the capital city of a nation which has felt more at ease in the country than in the town and has moulded its architecture and planning accordingly. At the most obvious level, this has led to the multiple versions of *rus in urbe* represented in the third chapter of this book: parks, gardens, leafy squares, city farms. Less visibly, it has resulted in large tracts of London being developed as 'estates'. Belgravia, Bloomsbury, Marylebone and Fitzrovia all grew up on the land of a few noble families who found that houses were a more profitable crop than any other. The effect of such development has been to preclude the monarchical grand gesture: it has helped to create a city which, like natural landscape, is composite not centralized and coheres more by virtue of underlying patterns than a visible geometry.

It is typical, too, that it took less than a week for Wren's plan for rebuilding burnt-out London to be drawn up, entertained by Charles II and rejected. Wren wanted to give London orderly public spaces and a geometric plan, but his ideas conflicted with property interests which the King knew he could not oppose. Had Wren's plan been built, its spaces would doubtless have become a favourite subject for painters. What Wren actually built were the dome of St Paul's and the many church spires that were to look so good from bridges and hills and were to compose themselves so well for Canaletto. Other monuments have followed Wren's lead, in contributing more to the skyline than the street: the Houses of Parliament, Tower Bridge, the British Telecom Tower. Now, when advertisers or newspapers want to represent London with a graphic, they usually amalgamate these monuments into a single silhouette.

The landscape and the wide view may have proved the best way of capturing London's diffuseness in two dimensions, but it is also a city particularly friendly to the written word. Shortly after the panorama painters tried to comprehend the city's enormity with their art, the likes of Thackeray and Dickens made it into fiction. The English are better at literature than any other art, and the structure of their capital is a narrative one. It is a city of plots and episodes, and its fabric recounts the ambitions, inspirations and absurdities of the people who have made it. The tower of Canary Wharf – a work of ambition, inspiration *and* absurdity – is only the latest such episode.

The greatest of London's narratives is the river, as Dickens recognized in *Our Mutual Friend*. The novel opens memorably with the Thames, as *Bleak House* opens with fog, and it provides the grisly livelihood of the heroine's father. The plot revolves about a body he fishes out of the water and the river both causes the death of a villain and is the setting for a beatific wedding. The Thames is also London's most impressive natural phenomenon and it is crossed by the bridges that provided such popular sites for easels and tripods. It is with the river that this book of panoramas and words starts.

THE RIVER

WITHOUT THE THAMES, London would not exist. There would have been no obstacle for the Romans to bridge, and so no fort to defend that bridge. There would have been no Pool of London to foster the city's early development, and no broad lower river to accommodate what became the greatest port in the world. Without its port, London would never have acquired the financial centre that is now its principal source of wealth and international standing. Even if it could exist, London without the Thames would have lacked its main thoroughfare, sewer, inspiration and playground. Dickens would have been deprived of his favourite settings and, without Monet's foggy riverscapes, London's contribution to Impressionism would have ended with Pissarro's views of South Norwood. There would have been no ice fairs on the frozen river, no Boat Race, and no Tower Bridge to put into blue plastic snowstorms.

All of which makes the modern Thames a bit of an embarrassment. With the closure of the docks it is, for the first time in London's history, redundant, and it is lined for much of its length with howling roads. In a crowded city it is a huge space that no one knows what to do with. There are desultory attempts to use it for passenger boats, and repeated suggestions for making it accessible, for dedicating its banks to something other than cars, but the will to implement them has not materialized. The latest, by Sir Richard Rogers, had the misfortune to be backed by the losing party in the last General Election. On the credit side, it is now at its cleanest for at least a century and a half, and its stink, which once forced parliament to abandon its business, has long since gone.

Most importantly, what survives contemporary neglect is a serene, magnificent natural event that provides the best key to understanding London. London is a narrative city, composed of sequences of events more than set pieces, richer in association and detail than spectacle, and the river is the greatest narrative of all. From its domesticated higher reaches, where it washes doorsteps and people sunbathe, to its broadening expanses as it approaches the sea, it unfolds plots and sub-plots of Chandleresque (or, indeed, Dickensian) complexity. It overlays the multiple private histories of those who made their living from the river and lived on it, with those of government, commerce, war and royalty. From Hampton Court to Greenwich, via Westminster and Whitehall, successive monarchs have established themselves along its banks, and few of the great monuments of secular and religious power – The Tower, St Paul's, Westminster Abbey, Parliament – are far away.

The river contains all London's moods and qualities, from charming domesticity to the muscular pursuit of trade, and all its fluctuations of weather and light. It combines the noble repose of Wren's compositions at Greenwich and Chelsea, with the achingly ugly, but still awesome dereliction of abandoned docks and industry. It also gives the most impressive views in London. From nowhere can you better sense the sheer might of the capital than from Waterloo Bridge or Tower Bridge.

HOUSE BOATS. CHELSEA WHARF

ART CENTER COLLEGE OF DESIGN

As bribes go, Cardinal Wolsey's donation of Hampton Court to Henry VIII must be among the largest and least successful in history. Hampton Court was then the most magnificent house in England, and Wolsey was trying to remain the King's most favoured counsellor. With his usual charm, Henry accepted the gift, dispensed with Wolsey, and set about making it still more splendid.

The battlemented Tudor portion of Hampton Court still recalls the medieval castle, but no one could expect its brick walls (brick, amazingly, was then a precious material) and large windows to withstand an attack. It represents a late idea of chivalry in the same play-acting spirit as the jousting and exotic costumes at the Field of the Cloth of Gold.

The seventeenth-century addition was commissioned by William and Mary, and, with its avenues of clipped trees, is as near as British royalty got to emulating Versailles, which is not very. Wren's stone-dressed brickwork is almost homely in comparison.

RICHMOND HILL

Richmond, like Hampton Court and much of the surrounding area, originally owed its importance to noble and royal patronage. Where Henry VIII used Hampton Court as a retreat from the unhealthy capital, Richmond was favoured by his father Henry VII. Henry was Earl of Richmond (in Yorkshire) before he took the throne, and gave the name to his palace on a site that had been popular with royalty throughout the Middle Ages. Now it describes one of the more convincingly rural suburbs, with the largest urban park in England and cows grazing in verdant riverside pastures.

CHISWICK MALL

In its unembanked upper reaches, the Thames enjoys a rather less formal relationship with the city than it does in the centre of London. Here the river will sometimes flood the roads at its edge and wash the doorsteps of houses, while at low tide it beaches boats, and allows you to walk about on its bed. This particular spot is two blocks away from the Great West Road, the principal route to Heathrow Airport, but preserves the appearance of a small, predominantly eighteenth-century, riverside town. It is much as it was when Thackeray chose it as the setting for Miss Pinkerton's Academy for Young Ladies, with which he opens *Vanity Fair*.

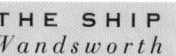

The riverside pub is one of the few places in central London which actively addresses the river. Otherwise the Thames is treated like a rich uncle, as something to be admired and exploited, but not to get too close to. The choice of site of this particular pub is, at first sight, surprising. It is just down river from the estuary of the Wandle river, which Isaak Walton found 'fishful' but has become considerably less so with the coming of some large gasworks (in this view, a gasometer is visible to the left of the boat's rigging) and other industry. One of these de-fishing industries, however, is the brewery of Young and Co., for whom the pub is an outlet. Industry, what is more, is leaving the area (as the emptiness of the river suggests), which makes it an ever better place to have a drink.

ART CENTER COLLEGE OF DESIGN

The tower block, wrecker of skylines and favourite tool of misguided post-war council housing, is the most execrated building type of our time. Strange, then, that the property boom of the eighties should rediscover the joys of high rise living. Chelsea Harbour, a development of flats and shops built round a marina, includes the first residential tower block to be built in London since the early seventies. The model, presumably, is Manhattan rather than council housing, and the flats were priced accordingly. Despite its name, it can only very tenuously be described as being in Chelsea: high property prices can make desirable place names very elastic.

ALBERT
BRIDGE

Until 1750 London only had one bridge,
London Bridge, and it was not until the
mid-nineteenth century that bridges were
built in any number. This accounts for the
pronounced differences, and mutual dis-

dain, between North and South London. Londoners tend to be loyal to one or other side of the river, but not both.

Albert Bridge, built in 1873, links Chelsea and Battersea, which are quite unalike. Chelsea feels like a place with a history; Battersea is a more homogeneous Victorian suburb. The bridge itself, which Pevsner sternly describes as 'prolix', is difficult either to take seriously or dislike.

As a suspension bridge, it can be grouped with heroic works of engineering like the Clifton Suspension Bridge in Bristol or the Golden Gate in San Francisco, but there is nothing heroic about its candlestick towers, its fairy lights, or its pastel colours. As one heads up river, it is a sign that the business-like centre is giving way to suburban eccentricity.

———————

Not everyone has heard of Sir Giles Gilbert Scott, but everyone in Britain knows his work. Here are his two most famous creations: Battersea Power Station (in the background) and the red telephone box. For fifty years the latter was a recurring sight throughout the country until, in the 1980s, British Telecom replaced most of them and sold them off. Many ended up as shower cubicles in interior-designed apartments across the globe. Some 2,000 remain in situ and retain their original purpose, as a result of being hurriedly listed as historic buildings and protected by law when BT's intentions became known. The listing process favours antiquity and rarity as well as aesthetic merit, which means that the older K2 design shown here has survived better than its later refinement, the K6, which was formerly more common.

This view of telephone box and power station is taken from a third work of embellished function, Albert Bridge.

ROYAL HOSPITAL
Chelsea

Started in 1682, the Royal Hospital at Chelsea was the first large royal building project after the Great Fire. Its purpose was (and is) to care for retired soldiers from the regular standing army, which had then been in existence for barely three decades.

Architecturally it combines several building types at once. The institution was inspired by Louis XIV's much grander Invalides in Paris, but this is a more domesticated, anglicized version, that in places resembles an oversized rectory. John Evelyn, who was involved in the project, compared it to 'a college or a monastery', though it also recalls barracks, is called a hospital and functions as an enormous almshouse. Its U-shaped plan, with a court facing the river, follows palace design of the period and every summer it fills with tents to serve yet another function, as the venue for the Chelsea Flower Show. If all this suggests a cacophony it is rather, as Carlyle said, 'quiet and dignified and the work of a gentleman', and its multiple allusions give an intriguing, enigmatic quality.

BATTERSEA POWER STATION

London is defined by a handful of buildings which, through their striking silhouettes, constantly assert themselves in views. St Paul's, Tower Bridge, the Lloyd's building and the BT Tower are members of this group: Battersea Power Station is another. Its value as a monument is greater than its use as a power station: completed in 1955, it had, at the time of its closure in 1983, for several years served only a single, if large, housing estate. Since then desperate attempts have been made to find new uses for this splendid but intractable object, and an abortive attempt to build an entertainment park round it has left it partly ruined.

For all the affection it now inspires, it came about through compromise and accident. Its architect, Sir Giles Gilbert Scott, was called in at a late stage to avert a monstrosity, and had wanted square, not round, chimneys.

(overleaf)

VIEW EAST FROM
MARKET TOWERS
Nine Elms

For a military intelligence organization, MI6 could hardly have chosen a less secret headquarters than Terry Farrell's enor-

THE PALACE OF WESTMINSTER

The Palace of Westminster is a building as paradoxical as the institution it serves, a constitutional monarchy. Just as Britain is governed by a curious combination of elected and unelected individuals, the Houses of Parliament is symmetrical and assymetric, Gothic and Classical, grand and domestic. No one should be surprised that it is the work of two architects.

The orderly planning of the building, and the rhythmic, almost Palladian, composition of the river frontage, is attributed to Sir Charles Barry, who, according to his son, 'would have preferred the Italian style'. The Gothic detail which unflaggingly covers the entire 11-acre building, inside and out, comes from the explosive talent of Augustus Pugin, the passionate advocate of Gothic architecture who died, insane, the year the building was officially opened. A Dr Reid should also be credited. Designer of the Palace's innovative heating and ventilation systems, its more fanciful turrets and spires were added, at his request, to serve as flues.

VIEW NORTH FROM JUBILEE GARDENS

On the left is the lugubrious Ministry of Defence with the winged Air Force memorial in front. Next is the bizarre Whitehall Court, a block of flats with the National Liberal Club attached, that seeks to out-château the most elaborate château of the Loire. After this the latest addition, Terry Farrell's Embankment Place, makes a determined bid to live up to such neighbours. Timorousness, it asserts, will not be one of its weaknesses. This building is a product of the eighties office boom, when it became profitable to build offices in the unlikeliest places, such as over railway stations, in this case Charing Cross. The curved roof is meant to evoke Charing Cross's long lost glass vault, and trains continue to issue from underneath, before crossing the river over Hungerford Bridge. On the extreme right is an earlier, equally assertive commercial monument, Shell-Mex House of 1931.

When the National Theatre (right) opened in 1976, it realized an idea first mooted by David Garrick in the eighteenth century, and campaigned for by Bernard Shaw. Opinions about Sir Denys Lasdun's architecture are divided, but the present author finds it magnificent. The play of light with shadow, of horizontal terraces stepping up from the river with vertical towers, has a power which London's often muddling architecture generally lacks. It is also a satisfying place in which to see plays, and in which the spectacle of the audience milling about its generous interiors matches that of the drama. Despite the fact that the heir to the throne has compared it to a nuclear power station, the theatre was renamed the Royal National Theatre in 1989.

The theatre occupies a pivotal site on a curve in the Thames, which looks towards Westminster in one direction and, in the other, towards St Paul's and the commercial monuments of the City.

In 1769 this was the third point in London
where the Thames was bridged, after London and Westminster Bridges. Now there
are two bridges: one of steel for trains and
another of stone for cars. Between them
they create one of London's more mysterious spaces, only glimpsed by most people
as they flash by on the road to the north.
Long and narrow, it is inhabited only by
the piers of an abandoned viaduct which,
medieval in detail and made of iron, seem
the remains of an inundated civilization.

To the south of the river, freed from the
restraints of high land values in the City,
modern office design becomes quirkier but
not necessarily better. The centre of the
three blocks seen here is the headquarters
of the *Daily Express*, which faintly echoes
the newspaper's old art deco building in
Fleet Street.

LONDON BRIDGE CITY

If the Emir of Kuwait saves London Zoo (see p. 110), this will not be the only mark his family will have left on London. London Bridge City (right), a huge commercial development that stretches between London's two most famous bridges – Tower Bridge and London Bridge – is the work of the St Martin's Property Corporation which, despite its Christian name, is owned by the Kuwaiti royal family.

HMS *Belfast*, moored in front of this array of office blocks is, despite appearances, yet another of London's museums. A survivor of the Second World War, it houses a museum of the Royal Navy, and is a favourite haunt of small boys.

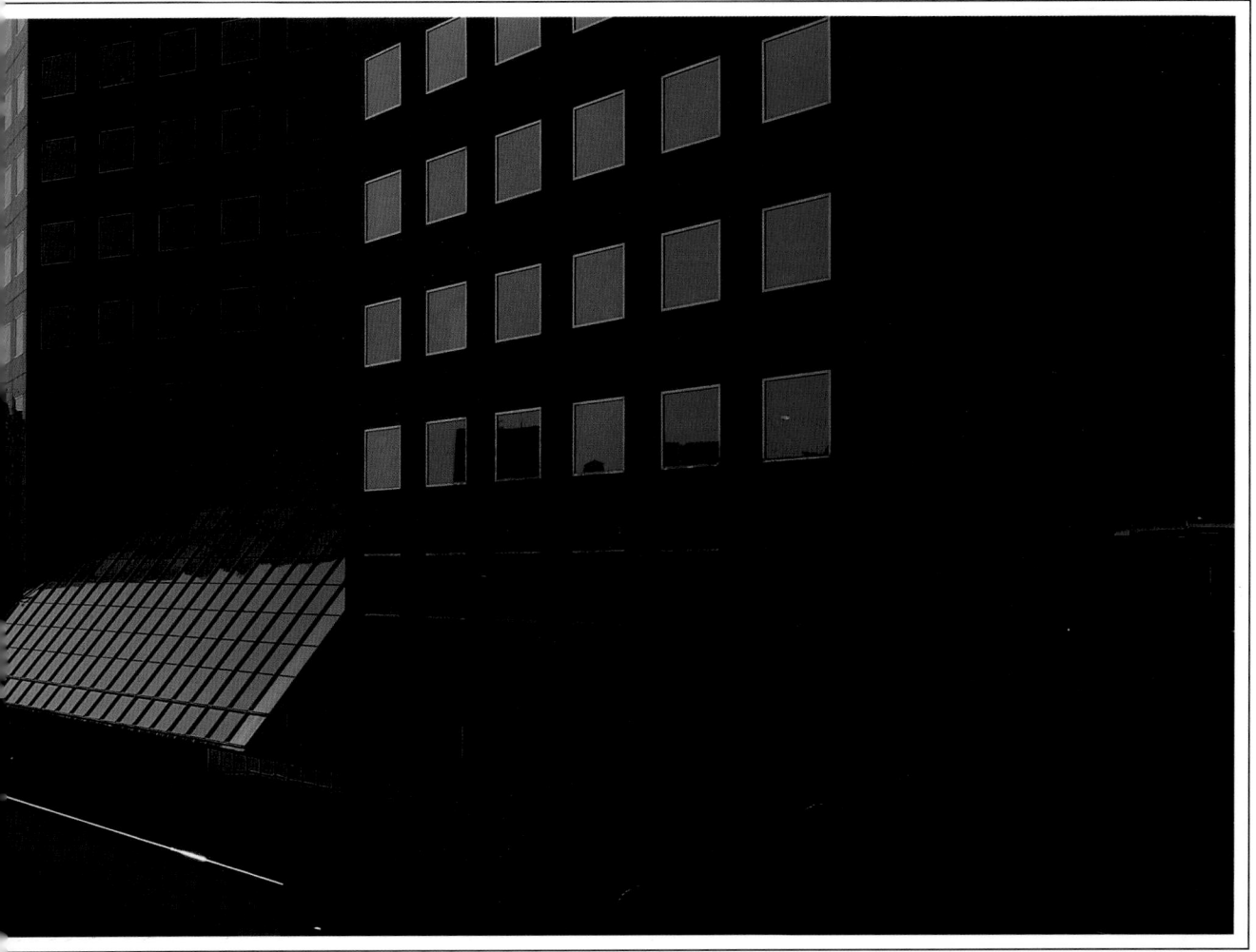

On the right are the highest land values in Britain. On the left is an area which, although it contained Shakespeare's Globe theatre, retains much of its recently industrial character. The bulky silhouette of Bankside Power Station is visible; by the same architect as Battersea Power Station, it is said by connoisseurs of such things to be better. Only forty years ago it was still going up, to the execrations of Sir Nikolaus Pevsner in his guide to London. Now threatened with demolition, people are clamouring for its preservation.

On the north bank, just left of the dome of St Paul's, the towers of Cannon Street station frame an office building built, as at Charing Cross, over the tracks. Further to the left is the slender white cone of Wren's St Bride. Just off Fleet Street, this has the thankless task of serving London's journalists, as godless a flock as one could imagine.

(overleaf)

SHAD THAMES

Georgian cities gave us terraces and pre-war suburbia the semi-detached; the contribution of the last two decades to domestic architecture is the warehouse conversion. As docks and industry ebb away from the world's great cities, and professionals flood in, what could be more logical than to hand the buildings of the former over to the latter? The attraction of warehouses is that they are usually nobly built, are often by water and, before developers crammed them with too many flats, had wide internal spaces. Since the genre was pioneered by artists in search of cheap space, they also have an attractive bohemian air. For all these reasons this view, which ten years ago would have been of a warehouse and a brewery, is now one of blocks of flats.

It also includes a museum. The white building on the extreme left is the Design Museum, opened in 1989, which makes this particular area the spiritual capital of the design-conscious warehouse dweller.

CANARY WHARF

Posterity will view Canary Wharf as an act either of vision or titanic folly. It certainly took courage, even in the boom years of its inception, to propose an immense office development (with a floor area one twelfth of the entire City of London) in the abandoned, ill-connected dockyards of the Isle of Dogs.

In a slump, the project has brought its developers low, but it has left London with the tallest, and one of the more dignified, towers in Britain, by the American architect Cesar Pelli. Simple in form, its stainless steel surface plays games with the shifting London light. At times the tower is a lowering presence, visible all over the capital; at others a brilliant orange sheet of reflected sunlight; at others still it is barely perceptible, and merges with the cloud.

On the horizon is Canary Wharf's rival, the City of London, and the National Westminster Tower, now Britain's second tallest building.

(overleaf)

Looking east towards the sea London's street pattern has finally given out, but the city's limits are still barely visible. Something more American has taken over: big roads, some big buildings, vacant spaces

between them, incongruity. To the left of centre Sir Richard Rogers's black and blue-grey technical centre for Reuters, the world's largest independent news agency, rises out of nothing. The orange pitched roofs of new housing try vainly, with forced jollity, to dispel the area's overwhelming toughness and emptiness. This was once one of the busiest stretches of water in the world; now it is clearly not.

In the middle distance the three parallelograms of water are the Royal Docks, the largest, most recent, and shortest lived of London's docks. The strip separating the two most distant docks is London City Airport and, to the right of them, the Thames Barrier stretches across the river. In the left foreground London's less celebrated river, the Lea, joins its sister.

Greenwich Hospital must be the grandest almshouse in the world. Built as a home for retired seamen on the site of a royal palace, it exemplifies a century's worth of England's best architects: Inigo Jones, Wren, Hawksmoor, Vanbrugh. Its composition achieves the symmetrical completeness striven for by royal palaces, like Hampton Court, but not achieved.

It is hard now to appreciate how startling Jones's demure, Italianate, white Queen's House seemed when new. Built for James I's wife, it could hardly differ more from the encrusted, turreted, bay-windowed palaces of the Elizabethans. It was also bizarrely planned. It was built in two parallel oblong blocks, connected by a bridge, astride what was then the Dover Road, so that the Queen could reach Greenwich Park without getting mud on her shoes. It came, unhappily for Sir Walter Raleigh's cloak, but luckily for picturesque myth, a little late: this was the spot where Raleigh made his famous sacrifice to Queen Elizabeth's footwear.

THAMES BARRIER

Far downriver, where the Thames starts to acquire a strong whiff of the sea, is London's most impressive and expensive work of twentieth-century engineering. It is also one which may never be needed, as it is designed to withstand a combination of wind and tide that may not happen. Since it was completed in 1982, its gates have been raised ten times, but only as precautionary measures, and the conditions against which it guards have not materialized. If they do, however, the barrier will amply justify itself, as it will protect London from a flood of unprecedented devastation, the cost of which, not including the cost in human misery, is conservatively estimated at £3,500 million.

An early initiator of the Thames Barrier project was Lord Waverley who, as John Anderson, gave his name to air raid shelters. This mitigator of apocalypse deserves to be made into some sort of secular patron saint of London.

THE TWO CITIES

THE greatest British virtue, and vice, is compromise. Tower Bridge is a compromise, between medieval architecture and Victorian engineering. St Paul's is a compromise, between the more perfectly centralized, symmetrical church Wren wanted, and the elongated nave his more conservative clients demanded. In politics compromise between crown and parliament takes the form of the constitutional monarchy. Centred about a powerless monarch it is one of the most absurd systems of government in Europe but also, over the last three hundred years, the most stable. This separation of powers is embedded in the structure of London, which is centred not on one city, but on two.

In Roman times the City of London, furnished with walls and a bridge, appears to have been the more important. The City of Westminster owes its status first to Edward the Confessor's decision to build a palace and a royal abbey there, and then to William the Conqueror's decision to be crowned there. From then on Westminster was the centre of royal power, the City of London of the rights of the citizenry. Even under absolute monarchy this was not a one-way relationship for, if the monarch had titular authority, the City had money, which it could barter for privileges and rights. On several occasions, when the succession was doubtful, the citizens of London had a decisive say in the choice of king. These rights are commemorated in ritual: the monarch has to ask permission to enter the City, and the ceremonies associated with the crown are approached in scale only by those associated with the Lord Mayor.

With the rise of parliament direct political influence ebbed from the City, and Westminster became the seat not only of the crown, but also of the Lords and Commons. The identities of the two cities have become no less distinct, but the distinction has been recast. Now the City is, almost exclusively, a centre of commerce and finance, served by a local government and police force adapted to its special needs. In terms of population it is the smallest city in England, having declined by 96% since 1851, but where in most cities this would be a sign of catastrophe, in the City it is a mark of its single-minded success. It remains a tight-knit place of small streets, well furnished with pubs and parish churches, but these now serve the daily inhalation of office workers rather than the few residents. The pubs close at weekends and the churches close on Sundays.

Westminster, by contrast, is a well-rounded city, endowed with theatres, museums, parks, hotels, department stores and places to live, as well as palaces and the institutions of government. Its more nebulous boundaries are not guarded, as the City's are, by heraldic dragons, and have been expanded over the years to include most (apart from the City itself) of what the word 'London' conjures, from Hyde Park to the Aldwych, and from the Tate Gallery to the Zoo. Without the City London would have much less money, but without Westminster it would be unrecognizable.

But the most important point is that neither can exist without the other. The British people may or may not find that they can dispense with the monarchy, but the centre of London will always be bi-polar.

THE ROYAL EXCHANGE AND THE BANK OF ENGLAND

THE CITY

It is from this point, just to the south of Tower Bridge, that the City of London most convincingly conveys its financial might. Framed between HMS *Belfast* on the left and the Tower of London on the right, its buildings impress not by being particularly tall (they are three times taller on Manhattan), but through their bulky solidity. They resemble some particularly immovable rock formation. However, this composition has not come about through market forces, but through the planning authorities of the 1960s, who decided that the most decorative arrangement of towers in the City would be a tall central one surrounded by a ring of stubbier acolytes. This is exactly what has come to pass.

It would be interesting to know if, in a few centuries' time, the Lubianka will be held in as much affection by the Muscovites as the Tower is now by Londoners. Although it was a place of torture and – up to and including the First World War – execution, it is now primarily associated with very long queues of tourists and Beefeaters, who must be among the world's least threatening soldiers.

It is the country's most prominent monument to the last time Britain was conquered, in 1066. It was also the prerequisite for London's growth: William the Conqueror built the central keep, the White Tower, both to awe his subjects and deter raids up the Thames. Under the Tower's protection the Pool of London became one of the world's great ports and the engine of the city's wealth. Without the Tower, it is quite conceivable that London would now be less significant than Winchester.

VIEW NORTH FROM THE MONUMENT

The day after the 1992 general election the largest terrorist explosion in London's history killed three people, destroyed most of a street in the City of London, and caused much damage over a wider area. The blast gave an alarming glimpse of how vulnerable London's self-confident financial centre could be. This view records the aftermath. Glossy commercial buildings are spotted with plywood panels where windows were blown out, and the Commercial Union headquarters – the square, black-topped tower in the centre – registers in white its missing glass.

In the face of such an event, architectural details seem irrelevant. For the record, the structure in front of the Commercial Union, bedecked with cranes and pipes, is Sir Richard Rogers's Lloyd's building, famous as London's most adventurous building of the 1980s. The institution it houses, Lloyd's the underwriters, also achieved notoriety in 1992, as heavy insurance losses drove several of its wealthy investors towards ruin.

LEADENHALL MARKET

In the past the City of London traded tangible commodities: meat, fish, vegetables. Now it deals almost exclusively in abstractions like corporate financing, currency speculation and shares. Leadenhall Market preserves a memory of the days when you could handle the goods transacted in the City. This was the site of the Roman Basilica, and of London's biggest market in the Middle Ages, and today it serves the needs of city workers out of open-sided shops. Its architecture is by the unsung master of Victorian solidity, Sir Horace Jones, author also of Tower Bridge, and Smithfield and Billingsgate markets.

(previous page)

SMITHFIELD AND THE CITY

One of the more startling juxtapositions in London is that between Smithfield meat market and St Bartholomew's Hospital, universally known as Bart's. The point is reinforced in the local pubs which have special licences to sell alcohol in the early morning, and sell visceral breakfasts to both blood-stained porters and surgeons as they come off their respective night shifts. The long, low roofs cover the market; the trees beyond are for the benefit of the patients of Bart's which, founded in 1123, is the oldest hospital in London. Beyond, on the right, is the dome of the Old Bailey, the most famous criminal court in Britain.

Both market and hospital have recently been threatened with removal, Smithfield by the economic forces which drove out the fish market at Billingsgate and the vegetable markets at Covent Garden and Spitalfields. The danger to Bart's comes from a government report which was concerned about the scantiness of local population it now serves. Both institutions, however, have so far proved tenacious.

This view depicts the City in its most
characteristic form: ordinary blocks,
medievally arranged, punctuated by
moments of distinction. Scanning the foreground from left to right, there are the two

shallow domes of Lutyens's Midland Bank, the column-ringed spire of Wren's St Mary-le-Bow (to the left of St Paul's), and the steep, gabled roof of the City's administrative centre, the Guildhall. Then

suddenly, there is London Wall, an unresolved meeting of post-war idealism and eighties excess. It is the only completed part of Route XI, a 1950s plan for a fast road, lined with an orderly row of widely spaced

towers. In the late eighties the City's planners, frightened that business would decamp to the well-appointed new offices of Canary Wharf, allowed the City's office stock to increase by about one sixth, and

London Wall bore the brunt. They need not have worried. At the time of writing both Canary Wharf and London Wall are distinctly under-occupied.

ST PAUL'S CATHEDRAL

The paving stones crossed by royal newlyweds, the bearers of distinguished corpses, and 1.5 million tourists a year. In Paris a boulevard or three would start here, and in Rome you would get a piazza, but here there is a curiously underwhelming, municipal space, bollarded and bounded by a road, and occupied by the white railed monument to an uncharismatic queen, Queen Anne. Its greatest assets are the fantastic towers and the lively, spring-like carving on the cathedral itself.

To the left are the sixties blocks of Paternoster Square, praised in their time, then reviled, and now threatened by bigger, ground-hogging blocks dressed in 'classical' façades. Faced with this work of thinly disguised greed, a few people are now asking whether the greater openness of the existing development is, after all, so very terrible.

For an object that is heard but almost never seen, Big Ben is remarkably famous. This is mainly because the large Victorian bell has transferred its name to the ornate, gilded structure that contains it, which is known to pedants and no-one else as the Clock Tower.

To the north the Houses of Parliament have spawned government buildings on the site of Whitehall Palace, once the largest royal palace in Europe but destroyed by fire in 1698. On the extreme right is the green-roofed Ministry of Defence. Clearly, its architect believed a bureaucratic building should be both forbidding and bland. Norman Shaw, however, designer of the red brick, turretted New Scotland Yard showed how even a police headquarters (as it was until 1967) could have a humane exterior. It is the architectural equivalent of the British policeman's helmet: it is dignified but a little absurd and so acts as a check on any power-fantasies the occupant/wearer might have.

(previous page)

WESTMINSTER ABBEY

The site of coronation since William the Conqueror, Westminster Abbey has grown up with the British monarchy and, like the monarchy, bears the mark of many influences over time. The Abbey enters recorded history as the work of the penultimate Saxon king, Edward the Confessor, who also started a palace here, and the building is a document of the succeeding nine centuries. It includes Saxon and Norman traces, rather more of French-inspired Gothic, Tudor extensions and a spiky skyline which, in spite of appearances, is hardly medieval at all. The twin towers are eighteenth-century and the pinnacles Victorian: again like the monarchy and its trappings, the Abbey is not all as antique as it appears.

TRAFALGAR SQUARE

The view most Londoners rarely get. Few brave the moat of traffic to reach the centre of the city's most famous square, and what can be, thanks to the fountains but no thanks to the pigeons, one of its more pleasant public spaces. The exception is New Year's Eve, when the square becomes the epicentre of a tumultuous throng that sends its tremors through most of the West End.

With the blasé attitude characteristic of British town planning, the square is composed of various buildings designed to only the vaguest overall plan, and by an approximate homogeneity. Out of the centre grows Nelson's Column, which, like most much-loved monuments, had to endure early derision: 'It is like a great stick or wand laid across a picture, and always marring the view of it', said *The Builder* in 1843.

Over the years theatre architects have found nothing more crowd-pulling than Baroque architecture and neon light. This is nowhere more evident than in Shaftesbury Avenue which, almost since its completion in 1886, has been the centre of West End theatre. Built as commercial ventures, its theatres jostle for attention like unusually glittering market stalls.

Commercial they still are. The subsidized theatres of the South Bank or the Barbican are the places for well-produced classics, and the cheaper theatres of the inner suburbs are more innovative, but the West End is still the capital of the lavish block-busting musical and the popular smaller show.

The joint work of a prince and an architect-developer, the Prince Regent and John Nash, Regent Street still bears the marks of a grand compromise between royalty and trade. The exigencies of early nineteenth-century real estate cause it to weave and wiggle, but it does so magisterially. Its breadth, and the formality of its quadrants and circuses, were, when first built, unmatched by anything in London.

After less than a century, however, it had become insufficiently grand for the commercial and imperial megalopolis that Edwardian London was, and saw itself to be. It was progressively rebuilt, with the doubled columns and fruity stonework of the Piccadilly Hotel, seen here, setting the tone. Now its character is a little neutral, borrowed from Piccadilly and Oxford Street, which it connects. It is less smart than one, and less sleazy than the other.

PICCADILLY ARCADE

Aristocratic ancestor of the shopping mall, the arcade reached London from Paris at about the time of the battle of Waterloo. A place sheltered from weather and traffic, conducive to lingering and people-watching, and with tiny, fragile-looking shops, the arcade has always tended towards the expensive and the rarefied. Now, compared with gigantism of stores elsewhere, the shops in London's arcades are more toy-like than ever, and glow more intensely with luxury.

Piccadilly Arcade, finished in 1910, is the last of the line, but it is a continuation of the first, Burlington Arcade, built in Lord Burlington's garden a century earlier.

(previous page)

35 LANGHAM STREET
Fitzrovia

Victorian London lacked two things: clean air and daylight. This is one response: a glistening, smog-proof, wipe-clean façade that penetrates the murkiest view and reflects light into the street, an astringent mouthwash applied to urban halitosis. Appropriately enough, it used to be a nurses' home, and it still crackles like starched linen.

Even when promoting hygiene, however, and when using an up-to-the-minute material like glazed brick, the late Victorians could abandon neither their obsession with grand architecture from the past, nor a leaning to the absurd. The arches and corbels recall a Romanesque cathedral; the patterning a print-out from a demented computer.

Buckingham Palace houses the head of a state rarely at ease with metropolitan life and, accordingly, it wishes it were a country house. Its rear looks onto large private gardens, its front and sides onto public parks. With a small effort, Range Rovers and people in headscarfs can be imagined at its doors.

The palace is not great architecture, nor is it meant to be, any more than the Queen's speeches to Commonwealth heads of government are meant to be great oratory. Like the monarchy, its qualities are predictability, reassurance and an appeal to a partly fictitious tradition: the main façade is thirteen years younger than the Queen Mother, but looks a century or so older. The palace faces a large round space, dominated by the water-girt memorial to Queen Victoria, which – usually a roundabout – becomes animated on royal occasions.

GREEN PARK

Green Park connects Hyde Park with St James's Park to form a virtually continuous string of green spaces from Parliament Square to Notting Hill Gate. It is smaller than Hyde Park, and lacks the theatrical landscaping of St James's, but its simple arrangements of mature plane trees on expanses of grass have a quiet nobility. Along with St James's Park, it was used by Henry VIII as a hunting ground. But although, in its woodier recesses, you can almost think yourself in the countryside, it is impossible to imagine deer and hounds rampaging through here.

———————

HYDE PARK CORNER

Constitution Arch is a doorway to nowhere in particular. It stands on what was, until the early nineteenth century, the western entrance to London – perhaps the last time when the City's edge could be clearly defined – but it now only punctuates the transition from Mayfair to Knightsbridge. Like its opposite number at the other end of Park Lane, Marble Arch, it was originally an entrance to Buckingham Palace and, like Marble Arch, is an example of the bizarre local sport of arch-moving: it came to rest in its present position in 1883.

Its other role was to commemorate the presiding hero of this corner of London, the Duke of Wellington, whose house, Apsley House, overlooks Hyde Park Corner. Constitution Arch once carried a statue of the general before the present statue of Victory, winged and drawn by four prancing horses, took his place. Since 1888, the Duke has been represented astride a less excitable beast. His granite plinth can be seen in the foreground.

VIEW EAST FROM THE LONDON HILTON

If a single view could contain modern London (which it can't), this would be it. It has the two cities — Westminster in front, the City beyond — and their representative monuments. Parliament and St Paul's. More modern landmarks punctuate the horizon: isolated on the left is Centre Point, once a notorious work of speculation but now beginning to inspire affection: just right of centre is the National Westminster Tower. Further to the right and in the far distance is the tallest of them all, the ever-present tower of Canary Wharf.

London's parks are well represented to the right by Green Park and St James's. To the left, the tree-filled Berkeley Square is another characteristic use of greenery. The view also intimates London's extent: even at this height you can't see its end. The hills on the extreme right, which from here seem completely undeveloped, punctuate rather than terminate the suburban spread, which continues on their far side.

(overleaf)

HOUSEHOLD CAVALRY
Knightsbridge Barracks

The life of a mounted guardsman is schizophrenic, divided as it is between wearing the most outrageous uniform in the British army, and careering about in the most modern tanks and armoured cars.

Like many of London's most famous 'traditions' the Household Cavalry, and the ceremonies at which they officiate, are part Victorian fabrication and part authentic. It is composed of regiments which, in the 1650s, took opposing sides. The Life Guards were formed by Charles II from his exiled supporters, while The Blues, since amalgamated with The Royal Dragoons, were a parliamentary regiment who, in 1660, switched their support to the returning King. The Household Cavalry might therefore be said to embody the historic compromise between crown and parliament that has governed Britain ever since. The Trooping of the Colour and the Changing of the Guard, however, are both theatrical inventions of the nineteenth century.

Although, in every sense except the administrative, the Royal Albert Hall is in Kensington, it is, officially, in Westminster. It was built, along with Imperial College and the South Kensington Museums, as part of the permanent fall-out from the Great Exhibition of 1851, held nearby in Hyde Park, and its round shape has been compared by different authors to 'Rome in its palmier days' and a bandstand. It also results in disastrous acoustics, which were only quite recently rectified.

Its use accordingly alternates between the sublime and the ridiculous. It houses some of the best music in London, tennis matches, boxing, and, in 1991, it became Europe's first Sumo wrestling venue. Each September, at the Last Night of the Proms, it exhibits in equal measure the British aptitude for queueing, ludicrous clothing and self-congratulation.

RUS IN URBE

LONDON is inhabited by a people not especially interested in cities, which makes it typical that the best book on London is by a foreigner. It also makes it typical that its most famous spaces contain trees, not buildings.

Writing in the 1930s for the edification of his fellow Danes, Steen Eiler Rasmussen, author of *London, the Unique City*, particularly admired both its open spaces and their used, rough quality, their muddiness, their emphatically un-Scandinavian scruffiness. He liked the fact that sheep grazed in Hyde Park (as they did then) and that people actually used parks for playing games rather than as untouchably neat pieces of gardening. He attributed London's proliferation of green spaces to the national passion for rolling about in mud. By these means, he argued, the Englishman released his primitive, child-like urges, which enabled him to be so famously buttoned-up, self-controlled and incorruptible the rest of the time. The absence of prostitution in the University towns of Oxford and Cambridge was due, he suggested, to the energetic open-air sports played by undergraduates.

The stereotypical Englishman he describes may have become less common in the last sixty years, but the evidence of history supports his thesis. The first open spaces to be protected by law were playing fields. Moorfields, used by the citizens of the City, was protected by progressively more stringent laws from 1478 on. Lincoln's Inn Fields, where law students held their sports, was protected from 1613. Sometimes violence was necessary: the open space at Red Lion Square was only saved from development after the people who played there fought building workers with bricks. At the top of the social scale, successive kings set aside huge areas for hunting, to which we owe the existence of the great royal parks.

But Londoners had other uses for parks. The riverside pleasure gardens of Vauxhall, Ranelagh and Battersea offered more licentious pleasures until the nineteenth century. Vauxhall, the most famous pleasure garden, would stay open until 3 a.m., and combined open spaces for fireworks, music and performances with densely wooded groves for private assignations. Of Battersea a Victorian missionary observed that 'if ever there was a place out of hell that surpassed Sodom and Gomorrah in ungodliness and abomination, this was it'. Inevitably, Victorian moral reformers took Battersea in hand and, doubtless to the delight and gratitude of all, replaced the 'comic actors, shameless dancers, drinking booths and unmentionable doings' with shrubberies, sub-tropical plants and what Rasmussen calls 'quite nice skiffs'.

Botany was another motive. In Chelsea and at Kew an interest in the medicinal properties of plants was combined with a fascination for getting into boats and gathering exotica from across the world. By the nineteenth century this had taken on an imperial tinge: ostensibly scientific and educational, Kew's collection of foreign flora mirrored the extent of Britain's possessions. During the same period other three-dimensional encyclopaedias were erected: the zoo for the world's animals and the Great Exhibition for the world's products. Part of the legacy of the latter is Monster Island, where the dominion of Victorian Britain is extended to the mesozoic age.

Now, in less arrogant times, the English love of the natural has taken yet another form. In depopulated areas city farms have grown up, *ad hoc*, modest shoestring operations which allow city children close contact with farm animals and which bring an improbably bucolic whiff to the most run-down areas.

SPITALFIELDS FARM

RUSSELL SQUARE

The London square is ostensibly urban, a direct descendant of the Place des Vosges in Paris. But it is also suburban, an early manifestation of the desire to live in the city and the country simultaneously that was later to find form in the garden suburb. The Place des Vosges is a public space and lined with arcades; the London square is frequently railed off, accessible only to keyholders, and its houses guard their privacy with impervious façades. Russell Square, the largest of London squares, has lost its austere Georgian unity to large hotels and some Victorian terracotta 'improvements', but its large garden (where the public *can* go) has majestic trees and a magnificent openness.

CHELSEA PHYSIC GARDEN

Although it lacks glistening apparatus and white tiles, the Chelsea Physic Garden was once a centre of advanced scientific research. It was founded in 1673 for the study of the medicinal uses of plants, and of their divine purposes – those which, it was believed, providence must have bestowed even on apparently useless flora. Under the patronage of Sir Hans Sloane (after whom Sloane Square is named) it became a centre of the explosion of scientific learning in late seventeenth- and early eighteenth-century England, as important in its way as the Greenwich Observatory or the Royal Society. It still contributes rare plant samples to the Natural History Museum and the pharmaceutical company Glaxo.

Since its foundation it has been the first port of call in Britain for successive waves of foreign plants, many of which have since become commonplace. Cedars of Lebanon made an early appearance here, and the garden includes the oldest rockery in Britain, made from Icelandic lava.

LITTLE VENICE

North and west of Paddington Station is an area of astonishing tranquillity, given that it is shaped by two millennia of transport engineering. To one side is the remorselessly straight Roman Watling Street. To another is Brunel's Great Western Railway, overlapped by the elevated Westway, the most infamous of the 1960s' grandiose traffic schemes. Through the middle runs the Grand Union Canal which, completed in 1820, runs through North and East London to join the Thames at Limehouse, and connects the London Docks with the national canal network.

The Canal's commercial usefulness was quickly eclipsed by the railways but, even when it was new, developers were drawn by the presence of water, and turned their handsome white houses to face it. Now this stretch is the Park Lane of waterways, offering the most desirable moorings in London to the residents of gaudy, flower-strewn narrow boats. It is hard to imagine the Westway, when obsolete, attracting such bijoux habitations.

Feeding Time 2.30 pm

PENGUIN POOL
London Zoo

Laid out in 1827, London Zoo now has only a shaky hold on life. At the time of writing, only the munificence of the Emir of Kuwait is staving off closure. Sheer lack of money is compounded by a decreasing confidence that it is beneficial to keep animals in cages.

If it goes, it will be a great loss to London. Divorced fathers will not know where to take their children at weekends, and Londoners will be deprived of those glimpses of the exotic that make life in cities worth living. There will also be the large and expensive problem of what to do with the menagerie of buildings which, like the Penguin Pool, are protected on the grounds of their architectural quality. Alternative uses do not spring to mind.

PRIMROSE HILL

Primrose Hill has a past less charming than its name. In the early nineteenth century it was a haunt for footpads and a venue for duels, and was then augmented by spoil from the digging of the nearby Regent's Canal. Now, rising surprisingly out of its flat surroundings it is a focal point for the residential areas of North London, a place to stroll on Sunday and take in the view. Lest its sprawlingness make them forget, residents of London can here remind themselves of the city to which they belong. A single view takes in almost all the big landmarks – Canary Wharf, St Paul's, the BT Tower, Westminster, and even the distant suburbs south of the river. The spectacle is sometimes accompanied by unearthly squawks from the birds in the aviary at London Zoo, which lies at the foot of the hill.

HAMPSTEAD HEATH

At Hampstead Heath, according to Steen Eiler Rasmussen, London made the choice between a park made for plants and a park made for people. Much of the flora, he points out, is impoverished and barren but 'in Hampstead we have in the middle of a great city an instance of the right preservation of Nature – *the human nature.*'

He was right. On Sundays, when people walk dogs, converse or fly kites against the backdrop of the capital, you get a stronger sense than anywhere else in London of people enjoying their city. But there are also, in the 700 acres of the Heath and its adjuncts, places where you cease to be conscious of London and you are left with fine trees and a gently undulating landscape. It is the combination of the two – the heightened awareness of both the city and its opposite – that makes Hampstead Heath a uniquely satisfying place.

(overleaf)

KENWOOD HOUSE

Kenwood is a typical English country house that happens to find itself enveloped by London. Its typicality takes several forms. It is the work of several generations, starting off as a seventeenth-century house that was embellished and added to by Robert Adam and others in the eighteenth century. It is itself orderly and symmetrical, but creates an irregular, 'natural' landscape about it through the careful placement of trees and water. What mattered was the illusion, not the actuality of the natural, a point emphasized by a 'bridge' which turns out to be two-dimensional scenery.

The house itself is scenographic, spreading its wings wide to increase its apparent size and omitting, as can be seen here, to carry the ornament of the central façade round the corner to its more functional side walls. Like other country houses it is no longer inhabited and is open to the public, who can view a large collection of paintings. What is rarer is that some of these are of exceptional beauty.

**VIEW EAST FROM
PARLIAMENT HILL**

Hampstead has always been one of the most desirable suburbs, for two principal reasons. One is the steepness of its hills, which kept out buses, trams and their vulgarizing effects; the other was the wish

f the Earls of Mansfield, who lived at Kenwood, to preserve their views unimpaired. To this Parliament Hill, until it was incorporated into the rest of Hampstead eath in 1889, owes its survival.

With its magnificent views over the city, it has become a favourite playground for North London. Even when looking east towards the less-than-splendid districts of Holloway and Finsbury Park, the rolling

landscape lends enchantment, and the domes and towers of their prosaic Victorian monuments acquire some mystery. Leigh Hunt, poeticizing about Hampstead, described 'A steeple issuing from a leafy

rise/With balmy fields in front and sloping green.' No poetic licence there, on the evidence of this view.

———————

The Victorians reformed many things: suffrage, prisons, drains — and cemeteries. Highgate is one of several suburban cemeteries built to relieve the congested churchyards of inner London, burdened still further by the victims of cholera epidemics. It is also the most famous, thanks to the presence there of what is left of Karl Marx.

Both Marx and the Victorian reformers imagined themselves to be informed by reason (what could be more reasonable than a sanitary new cemetery?), but the beauty of Highgate is the subversion of reason by intimations of the supernatural and of chaos. The (mainly) sensible tombs of bourgeois burghers assert a fragile stability against the organic menace of unkempt plants, slow ruin, and a shadowy, cloven landscape.

The park at Crystal Palace is a slightly mournful place, bereft of its eponymous monument: the Crystal Palace itself, moved here after the Great Exhibition of 1851, and destroyed by fire in 1936. It contains, however, one of London's most entertaining monuments to the fantastic. This is Monster Island, a piece of civic wilderness infested with life-size, multi-coloured, Victorian dinosaurs erected, allegedly, with educational intent. Progress in natural history has shown the models to be inaccurate, and their educational value is therefore nil, but the image of the prehistoric swamp in a leafy suburb continues to enthrall. Nearby, large bronze moose complete the incongruity.

HAM HOUSE

Ham House is a composite work of successive seventeenth-century owners, including William Murray, page and whipping boy to the young Charles I, whose reward for preserving his patience and good humour into adulthood included one of the smarter houses of the period.

The gardens, recently restored, were predominantly the work of a later owner, the Duke of Lauderdale, and were lavishly praised by Evelyn: they were 'inferior to few of the best villas in Italy itself: the house furnished like a great Prince's, the Parterres, Flower gardens, Orangeries, Groves, Avenues, Courts, statues, Perspectives, Fountains, Aviaries and all this at the banks of the Sweetest River in the World, must needs be surprising.' They include what is bizarrely known as the 'Wilderness', a geometric arrangement of clipped hedges seen here in the foreground. This, it would appear, was as wild as their designer, a German military engineer, was prepared to go.

ISABELLA PLANTATION
Richmond Park

The name suggests the deliberate act of a noble benefactress, but the Isabella Plantation owes its character to a 1940s municipal gardener (or gardeners) and its name, indirectly, to the colour of Isabella of Austria's underwear. She was a rash character who vowed not to change her linen until the siege of Ostend was successful. Since it took three years, her name came to describe 'a light yellowish-grey or drab colour' (Collins New English Dictionary) that is also the colour of the soil in this corner of Richmond Park. The origin of its planting, although recent, is obscure but it seems that the said municipal gardener observed that conditions in this little wood were ideal for rhododendrons, azaleas and other spectacularly un-drab plants. He and his successors exploited this fact with, as may be seen, riotous effect.

(previous page)

PALM HOUSE
Kew Gardens

First the private property of royalty then, from 1841, in the hands of the state, Kew has always been a centre of organic and architectural exotica. It was here that the first specimen trees were planted and, in the later eighteenth century, where Sir William Chambers led the reaction to the placid, some would say dull, landscape designs of Capability Brown. Chambers developed the 'sublime' landscape, which was more theatrical and fantastic. It was decorated with a mosque, an Alhambra, a Chinese Temple and a Pagoda, which survives. In the nineteenth century, science combined with Imperial pride to produce a permanent Great Exhibition of the world's plants. This included the most remarkable precursor of the Crystal Palace, the Palm House, which today gives the best idea of what was lost when the former burnt down.

VILLAGES AND EPISODES

LIKE all good truisms, the idea that London is a city of villages is true, but also extravagantly misleading. The truth lies in the fact that London is diffuse and centrifugal, and composed from the multiplication of distinctive sub-centres and, if some of the more recent suburbs are numbingly similar, London does include an astonishing diversity of districts. Camden Town, Primrose Hill, St John's Wood and Hampstead could all be encompassed in a not-too-demanding walk but each offers an utterly different combination of milieu, configuration, and architecture. Such sub-centres exist even in the heart of London, in Soho, Clerkenwell and the Inns of Court.

Many have the trappings of villages: greens, parish churches, a whiff of the rural, irregular roads that trace some ancient cart track. Many have local fairs, markets and fireworks displays. But all are marked by their proximity to the metropolis, with the unmistakably urban. Kensington, for example, was a village, and retains traces of its structure, but how many villages contain a Royal Palace and several museums? Other areas that were once genuine villages have long since been obliterated by the gigantic engineering of the last two centuries, by Victorian railways or 1960s roads. Thus St Pancras retains its medieval church and bucolic churchyard but has otherwise surrendered to railways, gasometers and the interminable building site that is the new British Library. To the west, the Westway has obliterated old patterns, but has created new, ad hoc spaces much loved by film makers.

Most importantly, almost no one now inhabits 'villages' as they would a real village. Few people rely on a particular district for shelter, society, work, entertainment *and* essential supplies, but only for one or two of these items at a time. Life in London is rather a matter of rapid, daily migration through different districts in pursuit of different ends. Like a politician seeking election, the city dweller will flit through several 'villages' a day. Each, briefly, will absorb his attention before he passes on. In the course of a lifetime the homeowning Londoner is likely to criss-cross the city with an unpredictable Brownian motion, impelled by the invisible forces of property prices and by the search for good schools or congenial neighbourhoods.

All this has remarkable effects. It means that the arteries of London – roads, trains and their intersections – are also its most effective public places, places of encounters and public events, both planned and otherwise. The places with the trappings of public space – squares, greens, the equivalents of marketplaces in country towns – commonly have an introspective, optional air. Individual districts, rather than forming coherent nuclei, are experienced as if they were episodes in a novel, vivid but transitory.

This might sound like a diminution, the trading of much-praised virtues like community spirit and continuity for fleeting sensation. But what has gone is not so much the idea of community as its link with a geographic location. London is composed of innumerable coherent, thriving communities but they are overlaid to form an inextricable tissue of networks, rather than a set of discrete, visibly bounded entities.

And, if London is composed of episodes, they can be spectacular ones. No operation of reason or the imagination could predict a city that holds, simultaneously, buildings like Christ Church Spitalfields, the Southwark Hop Exchange or the Michelin Building, which juxtaposes hospitals and meat markets as Smithfield does, or where turning a corner can plunge you into Hong Kong, Dacca, Port of Spain or County Kerry.

HOLLAND PARK

THE HOP EXCHANGE
Southwark

The Hop Exchange survives from the days when London dealt more directly in material commodities, rather than their electronic ciphers, than it does now. Well placed for the hop fields of Kent to the south of the City, it is also a magnificent building. Disregarding classical properties, its blue, iron colonnade in the Composite order simply carries on until it is time to stop. This, and the vaguely Venetian upper storeys, are carried off through sheer verve. Its great sweep is punctuated only by the pedimented entrance (wholly inadequate in classical terms) which is decorated with very literal depictions of the farming and trading of hops.

In London's more relaxed suburbs, the garden becomes a public art. Even the narrowest strip of land becomes a showcase for its owner's skill and enthusiasm, and variety, it seems, counts for more than chromatic harmony. The houses, too, unbutton, and the regular terraces of inner London give way to a more intimate scale, and varied compilations of colour, material and detail.

The firewood is technically illegal in what, equally technically, is a smokeless city. However, with the passing of the lethal smogs that gave rise to London's Clean Air Acts, they are not vigorously enforced. Now the worse threat is from car exhausts, not domestic fires.

ST PANCRAS
AND GASOMETERS

The British often produce their most powerful architecture when they think they are doing something else, like engineering. Hence the gasholders on the right, started in 1824, still in use, and now protected as

historic buildings. Large, uninhabited, circular structures, open to the sky, were once confined to prehistoric religious sites like Stonehenge or Avebury. These functional objects retain a mysterious aura.

To the left is more engineering, the impressive train shed of St Pancras station, which was once the widest spanning roof in the world. It is decorated at its far end by the 'architectural' pinnacles and spires of

George Gilbert Scott's Great Northern Hotel, which has been less respected by posterity than the train shed. Between the train shed and the gasholders is the slender cylinder of the BT Tower. Again, it is

primarily engineering – its peculiar shape comes from the logistics of positioning transmission equipment – but, once derided, it inspires increasing affection.

———————

THE PARAGON
Blackheath

In the past Blackheath was a favourite gathering point for various types of horde, usually with ill intent towards London. In 1011 it was invading Danes, in 1381 and 1450 revolting peasants. In 1497 Henry VII fought here with Cornish rebels. In the nineteenth century Blackheath fair was hugely popular, despite being banned by Act of Parliament.

In spite of this Blackheath was also, in the eighteenth century, a favourite retreat for the better off. Where other such places — Highbury, Hackney — have been engulfed, it still retains an airy openness and calm. It also retains the Paragon, a late eighteenth-century development overlooking the Heath, composed of some of the grandest semi-detached houses in existence.

ST PETER'S SQUARE
Hammersmith

By the time St Peter's Square was built, in the 1820s, the London square was nearly two centuries old. The first, Inigo Jones's Piazza at Covent Garden was imposing and at the centre of things; here the idea has migrated to the suburbs and become less formal, and more private. Where Jones's Piazza had public arcades, St Peter's Square has front gardens and, where one had high architecture, the other has stucco columns, ornamental pineapples and sleepy lions, that cannot be taken entirely seriously.

As a genre, the square has not, by this time, long to live. The original idea was to unify houses behind palace-like façades, but here they reassert their individual identities. The time is not all that far off when they will break up into villas and semi-detached pairs.

HIGHBURY
TERRACE

When it was built in 1789, Highbury Terrace stood in open countryside, a quiet but convenient retreat for the prosperous. Its plain, urbane façade and broad pavement, standing amid agriculture, must have been a strange sight, but it was not to last. A wave of meaner, rougher Victorian houses engulfed the area and a further blow to its gentility was the arrival of Arsenal Football Club between the wars. On Saturdays the crowd's roar now resounds, to their mute surprise, about the Georgian bricks and railings. However, these and nearby terraces overlook Highbury Fields, a sloping, green, open space. Together with the dignity of the architecture, this has lately attracted back into the area those of the professional classes who are not too snobbish about location.

Wandsworth has changed since, in 1776, it was a village of 'many handsome seats . . . belonging to the gentry and to those citizens who have retired from the fatigues of business'. Since then it has become a typical Victorian suburb, created by trains and trams, with row upon row of brick-and-slate terraced house, each with its own modest garden. Now it is Blondtod-dlerland, inhabited by reasonably prosper-ous, reasonably young couples and their fair offspring, who are much in evidence on its pavements.

TRINITY GREEN ALMSHOUSES
Stepney

The architecture of Chelsea Hospital (see p. 28) in miniature. Completed four years later than Chelsea, it was built for '28 decayed masters and commanders of ships or the widows of such'. It is occasionally alleged, without much foundation, to be by Wren but it is clearly influenced by his combinations of red brick and white stone and has a Chelsea-like plan of domestic wings flanking a central chapel. Again like Chelsea, it is open on its southern end, but it faces Mile End Road, which is rather less manicured and rather more noisy than the lawns at Chelsea. This, however, makes the tranquillity of its little courtyard all the more wonderful.

Attached but apart, Chiswick House sits in relation to Chiswick in much the same way as grand houses do to villages in the real countryside. It was, however, both less and more than a country seat. Designed in 1725 by Lord Burlington for himself, it was used as a place of entertainment and reflection, as an occasional retreat from the capital, rather than the centre of local power. At the same time it was a hugely influential architectural manifesto, a display of the Italianate learning and taste Burlington brought back from his Grand Tour. Its motifs can be found on stately homes built over the ensuing century up and down the country, and it is the representative building of English Palladianism, which is what most English people think of if they talk about 'classical' architecture.

(overleaf)

SPITALFIELDS

Crossing Bishopsgate, one encounters one of the most abrupt transitions in London. On one side are the titanic office blocks from the eighties building boom, on the other Spitalfields, one of the most ramshackle but intense areas of London. Ever since the seventeenth century it has been both the centre of the rag trade and the destination of successive waves of immigrants—first Huguenots, then Jews, and now Bengalis — and the area is now dense with sweatshops, and suffused with the sounds and smells of the Indian sub-continent.

All this takes place among streets which, beneath their dereliction, preserve their early Georgian dignity. In their midst is Hawksmoor's Christ Church (right), a sepulchral white pile, part Roman, part Gothic, of astonishing majesty and invention. At such time as the sums add up, the area in the foreground is to be redeveloped, and the frontier between offices and the rest of the world will move east, but it will take more than one mega-development to eradicate the character of this area.

— 1 5 3 —

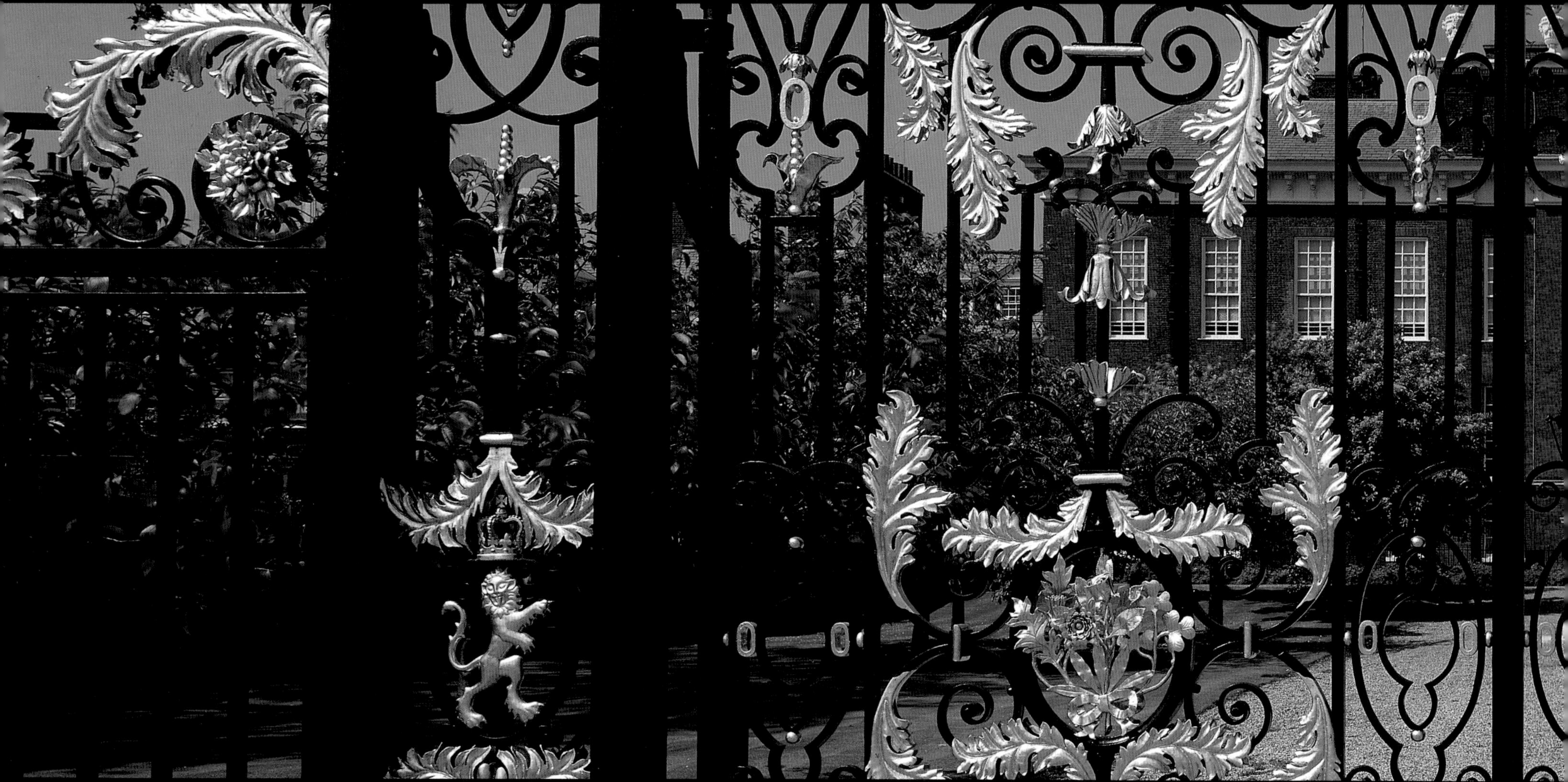

KENSINGTON
PALACE

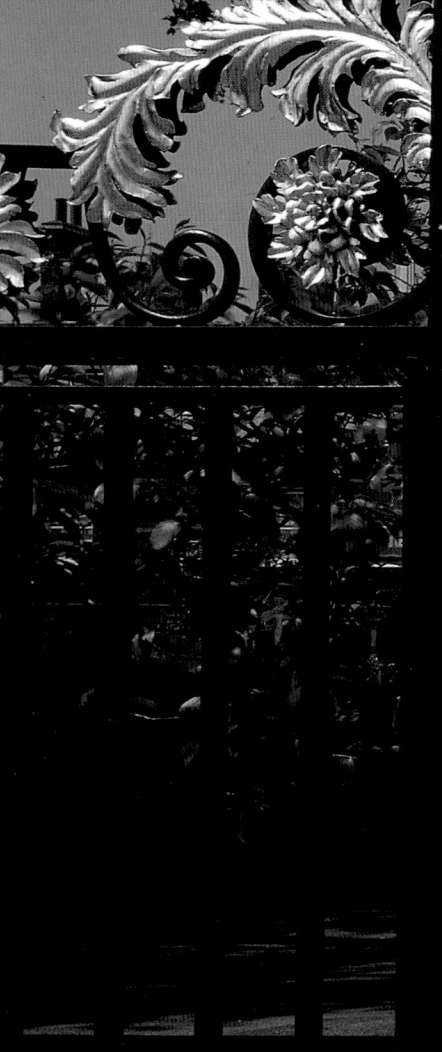

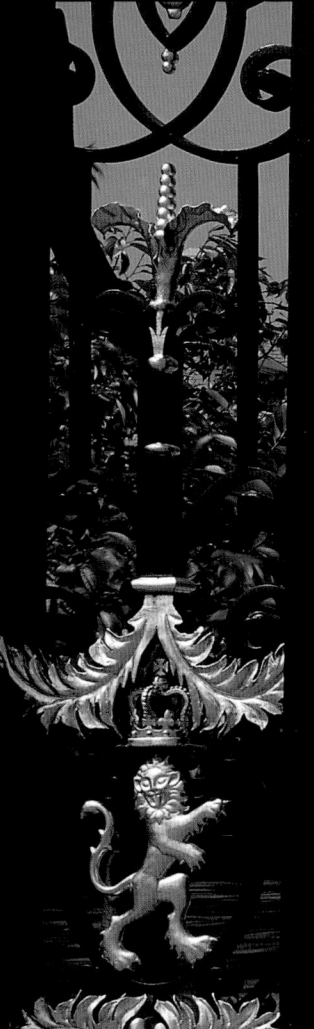

Little can have had more effect on London than William III's bronchitis. It drove him to abandon Whitehall Palace, then the largest in Europe, and donate Greenwich to old sailors, and retreat to the purer air of

Hampton Court and Kensington. Since his eventual cause of death was a molehill (on which his horse tripped), he need not have bothered but, in Kensington, the King's move generated a new suburb to house courtiers and hangers-on. Kensington still has an elevated standing, and it is a favourite habitation for the modern, international successors to courtiers – ambassadors and their staff.

The palace itself is a monument to a domesticated monarch. No one in possession of a Divine Right would build anything like this. 'The comparison with Versailles or Schönbrunn', as Pevsner says, 'makes Kensington Palace look pitiable', but Kensington succeeds instead at being agreeable and unoppressive.

The Michelin company has given much more to western culture than just tyres: guides, culinary ratings, and the most unmitigated moment of sheer pleasure in London's architecture. Its multicoloured, tyre-inspired tilework imbues the building with the *bon vivant* spirit of Michelin's pneumatic hero, Bibendum, who looms benignly from the stained glass. Appropriately enough, Bibendum now has a restaurant named after him, installed as part of the building's recent revamp. The rear section now contains The Conran Shop, which sells contemporary furniture, and the Michelin building as a whole is the focus of a gathering of highly designed shops and restaurants in the adjoining streets.

ACKNOWLEDGEMENTS

The author, photographer and publishers would like to thank the following individuals, companies and institutions for their advice and kind assistance: Alistair Aitken, Chelsea Physic Garden; William Broadbent, Warwick Balfour Properties PLC; Anne Carman and Christopher Clarke, Westminster School; Gary Chapman and Terry Archer, Russells Colour Laboratories; Hampton Court Palace; Richard Lane, Knight Frank & Rutley; David Larkin, Jones Lang Wootton; The London Hilton; London Zoo; Shaun Longsdon, Knight Frank & Rutley; New Zealand House; Brian O'Connor, Debenham Tewson & Chinnocks; Jean Pateman, Friends of Highgate Cemetery; Lella Raymond and Julian Scantlebury, Trinity Green; Royal Botanic Gardens, Kew; Royal Parks.

The photographs of Kenwood (pp. 116–7) and Chiswick House (pp. 150–1) appear with the kind permission of English Heritage; Ham House (pp. 124–5) with the kind permission of the National Trust.

Photograph of the Household Cavalry (pp. 96–7) by kind permission of Col Jeremy Smith-Bingham, Lt Col commanding the Household Cavalry.

It has been a great pleasure to work with Alice Millington-Drake and Emma Way for which the author and photographer thank them.

INDEX

Page numbers in *italics* refer to illustrations

Text copyright © Rowan Moore 1993
Photographs copyright © Sampson Lloyd 1993

First published in Great Britain in 1993 by
George Weidenfeld & Nicolson Ltd
Orion House, 5 Upper St Martin's Lane,
London WC2H 9EA

British Library Cataloguing-in-Publication Data
A catalogue record for this book is available from the
British Library.

Phototypeset at The Spartan Press Ltd,
Lymington, Hants
Colour separations by Newsele Litho Ltd
Printed and bound in Italy

Edited by ALICE MILLINGTON-DRAKE
Designed by PETER BRIDGEWATER

ENDPAPERS: *Park Crescent, Regent's Park*
PAGE 1: *Cloth Fair, Smithfields*
PAGES 2–3: *View east from London Bridge*
PAGES 4–5: *View west from Canary Wharf Tower*
PAGE 6: *Richmond Park*
PAGES 10–11: *Sunrise over the City*
PAGES 56–7: *View east from New Zealand House*
PAGES 100–101: *View west from the London Hilton*
PAGES 130–1: *Fair on Wimbledon Common*